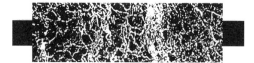

MOTIVATION

LOMBARDI
STYLE

CELEBRATING EXCELLENCE PUBLISHING

Book Design: Michael McKee and Judith Orr

ISBN: 1-880461-27-7

4 5 6 7 8 Printing/AK/Year 98 97 96 95 94

MOTIVATION

LOMBARDI
STYLE

Table of Contents

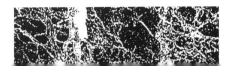

Introduction

"Leaders are made; they are not born."

Vince Lombardi believed that the ingredients of greatness are not necessarily inherent traits, but rather qualities to be encouraged and cultivated. Through his "total dedication" to the heights of human potential, football's legendary coach created champions.

Lombardi's spartan approach to motivation helped transform the Green Bay Packers of the early 1960's from perennial losers to unrivaled contenders. Little known, even second string team members, such as Bart Starr, became national superstars under his driving influence. Two Super Bowl victories to his credit, Lombardi left football in 1967, only to return two seasons later and lead the Washington Redskins to their first above par performance in more than a decade. With the power to turn around teams and keep winners on top, Lombardi applied the basic principles of motivation much like the football fundamentals that won a record number of games.

Discipline, intensity and sacrifice were among the convictions that dominated his own life and that of anyone with the talent and tenacity to play for him. Both admired and feared, Lombardi could arouse strong emotions and elicit decisive results. Using keen insights, clever anecdotes and unyielding intimidation when necessary, he forced players to exceed their physical and mental limitations.

Likewise, the meaning and importance of Lombardi's lessons transcended sports. He recognized the many correlations between the game of football and the game of life; the athletic playing field and the business battlefield.

Vince Lombardi believed that no matter what the endeavor, desire, not ability, determines success. It was his own passion for excellence that made his an extraordinary leader whose greatest victory may well have been in winning over the hearts and minds of countless individuals.

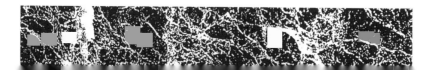

BELIEF

"A man can be as great as he wants to be. If you believe in yourself and have the courage, the determination, the dedication, the competitive drive and if you are willing to sacrifice the little things in life and pay the price for the things that are worthwhile, it can be done."

— *Vincent Lombardi*

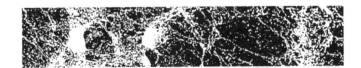

2

"Coach Lombardi was a super salesman, one of the finest salesmen there's ever been. He has a knack for selling himself and his system ...He's able to do this because, first, he believes passionately in what he's selling—in himself and his system. And, second, he's a great teacher, both on the field and on the blackboard."

— *Bart Starr*

3

"**H**e made us realize that if the mind was willing, the body can go."

— *Forrest Gregg*

"**U**nless a man believes in himself and makes a total commitment to his career and puts everything he has into it—his mind, his body and his heart—what is life worth to him? If I were a salesman, I would make this commitment to my company, to the product and most of all, to myself."

— *Vincent Lombardi*

"He never compromised. There was only one way and that was his."

— *Tom Landry*

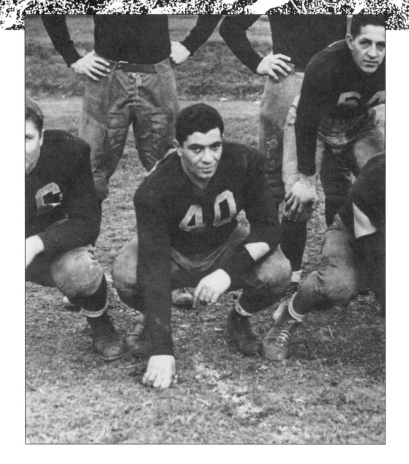

"He made you a believer. He told you what the other team was going to do, and he told you what you had to do to beat them, and invariably he was right."

— *Willie Davis*

5

"He made us all better than we thought we could be."

— *Jerry Kramer*

"He was a master at handling and inspiring us. He's the kind of man you just have to win for."

— *Paul Hornung*

"A man who is trained to his peak capacity will gain confidence. Confidence is contagious and so is lack of confidence and a customer will recognize both."

— *Vincent Lombardi*

COMMITMENT

"The quality of a person's life is in direct proportion to their commitment to excellence, regardless of their chosen field of endeavor."

— *Vincent Lombardi*

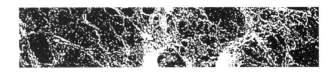

"He never missed a
practice. Never.
There were times
when he went to
bed with a high
temperature and
woke up with an
even higher one.
I'd tell the doctor,
'There's no way
you're gonna keep
him off the practice
field today,' and the
doctor would say,
'I know.'"

— *Marie Lombardi*

9

"This is not easy, this effort, day after day, week after week to keep them up, but it is essential."

— *Vincent Lombardi*

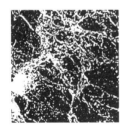

"Once a man has made a commitment to a way of life, he puts the greatest strength in the world behind him. It's something we call heart power. Once a man has made this commitment, nothing will stop him short of success."

— *Vincent Lombardi*

"He pushed you to the end of your endurance
and then beyond it. And if there was reserve there,
well he found that too."

— *Henry Jordan*

"I demand a commitment to excellence and
to victory and that is what life is all about."

— *Vincent Lombardi*

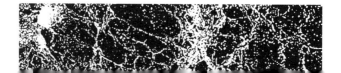

12

"Leaders are made, they are not born. They are made by hard effort, which is the price which all of us must pay to achieve any goal that is worthwhile."

— *Vincent Lombardi*

"You had to stand up and do what was demanded of you. If it was windy, he wouldn't accept the wind as an excuse or if the ground were frozen you weren't allowed to slip. You had to adjust. He never said, 'That would have been a good pass except the wind was bad.' Never."

— *Zeke Bratkowski*

"**A**ll he wanted from
you was perfection."

— *Jim Taylor*

"**I**t's not

whether you

get knocked

down, it's

whether you

get up."

— *Vincent Lombardi*

15

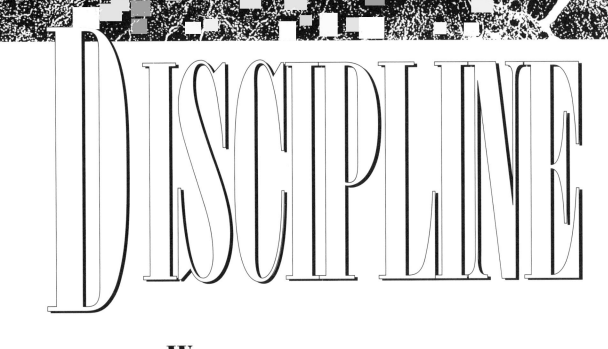

DISCIPLINE

"We did everything on Lombardi Time. Once, in pre-training camp, a receiver showed up for a meeting five minutes early, which meant he was really ten minutes later than everyone else. Coach Lombardi jumped on him. 'Young man,' he said 'you'll never play for me if you can't be on time.' That fellow didn't make the team, either."

— *Sonny Jurgensen*

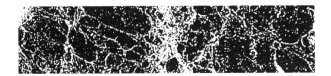

16

"Coach Lombardi showed me that by working hard and using my mind, I could overcome my weakness to the point where I could be one of the best."

— *Bart Starr*

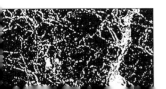

"He told us, 'The Good Lord gave you a body that can stand most anything. It's your mind you have to convince.'"

— *Ken Iman*

18

"I've never known a man worth his salt who in the long run, deep down in his heart, didn't appreciate the grind, the discipline. There is something good in men that really yearns for discipline."

— *Vincent Lombardi*

"I think that a boy with talent has a moral obligation to fulfill it, and I will not relent my own responsibility."

— *Vincent Lombardi*

"**M**ental toughness is many things and rather difficult to explain. Its qualities are sacrifice and self-denial. Also, most importantly, it is combined with a perfectly disciplined will that refuses to give in. It's a state of mind—you could call it character in action."

— *Vincent Lombardi*

"You teach discipline by doing it over and over, by repetition and rote, especially in a game like football when you have very little time to decide what you are going to do. So what you do is react almost instinctively, naturally. You have done it so many times, over and over and over again."

— *Vincent Lombardi*

PREPARATION

"Coach was very methodical in his approach—almost to the extent that it was boring. However, we knew what to do, when to do it and why we did it."

— *John Symank*

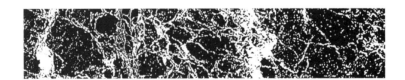

22

"**O**nce you have established the goals you want and the price you're willing to pay, you can ignore the minor hurts, the opponent's pressure and the temporary failures."

— *Vincent Lombardi*

23

"Confidence comes from planning and practicing well. You get ready during the week and the confidence will be there on Sunday. This confidence is a difficult thing to explain. But you do get it and the team gets it if you have prepared properly."

— *Vincent Lombardi*

"They call it coaching but it is teaching. You do not just tell them...you show them the reasons."

— *Vincent Lombardi*

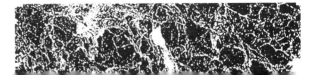

"Fundamentals win it. Football is two things: it's blocking and it's tackling. I don't care anything about formations or new offenses or tricks on defense. If you block and tackle better than the team you're playing, you'll win."

— *Vincent Lombardi*

"I think good physical conditioning is essential to any occupation. A man who is physically fit performs better at any job. Fatigue makes cowards of us all."

— *Vincent Lombardi*

"I don't think any team went into its game each Sunday as well prepared as we were. We knew just what to expect and we knew just how to cope with it."

— *Paul Hornung*

"As far as describing Vince as a coach, I wouldn't call him flamboyant or spectacular. He worked hard, of course, he drives himself—but I'd say the things he does are what everyone else does, only he does them better."

— *Sid Gillman*

26

"You might reduce Lombardi's coaching philosophy to a single

sentence: In any game, you do the things you do best and

you do them over and over and over."

— *George Halas*

"He made it explicitly clear what he wanted. He didn't leave anything to chance. He didn't leave any hesitation on your part. He just laid it out in black and white. And if you did that, even if you erred, if you did what he said he wanted, he would never be on you."

— *Bart Starr*

"We didn't concern ourselves as to what the elements were, the weather conditions. The point is, you've got to play and that's a fact of life. That's what you're here for. And the team that can function best under any conditions comes out victorious."

— *Willie Wood*

"He prepared us so well, and he motivated us so well, I felt he was a part of me on the field."

— *Fuzzy Thurston*

DESIRE

"The difference between a successful person and others is not a lack of strength, not a lack of knowledge, but rather in a lack of will."

— Vincent Lombardi

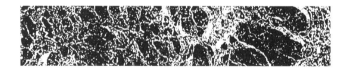

"**I**'d rather have a player with 50% ability and 100% desire because the guy with 100% desire you know is going to play every day so you can make the system to fit into what he can do. The other guy—the guy with 100% ability and 50% desire—can screw up your whole system because one day he'll be out there waltzing around."

— *Vincent Lombardi*

"The spirit, the will to win and the will to excel—these are the things that endure and these are the qualities that are so much more important than any of the events that occasion them."

— *Vincent Lombardi*

"He taught me that you must have a flaming desire to win. It's got to dominate all your waking hours. It can't ever wane."

— *Bart Starr*

"**I**f you're lucky enough to find a guy with a lot of head and heart, he's never going to come off the field second."

— *Vincent Lombardi*

"**T**he man was a perfectionist...he was never satisfied simply by victory. He always wanted us to play as well as we were capable of playing."

— *Bart Starr*

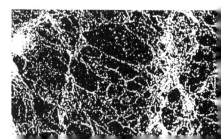

"It is essential to understand that battles are primarily won in the hearts of men. Men respond to leadership in a most remarkable way and once you have won his heart, he will follow you anywhere."

— *Vincent Lombardi*

"You couldn't believe how much he wanted to win the games that didn't count—those after we had clinched the division title."

35

— *Bill Forrester*

CHARACTER

"The strength of the group is in the will of the leader and the will is in the character of action. The great hope of society is the character of action. We are never going to create a good society, much less a great one, until individual excellence is once more respected and encouraged. If we will create something, we must be something. Character is the direct result of mental attitude."

— *Vincent Lombardi*

"It takes a special kind of character to know when to let up, when to back off. He would get them to the point when they were just about ready to do anything and then he was able to crack a joke or he was able to do something to break the tension and put them back on the right track."

— *Tom Landry*

37

"If I had to pick one reason for his enormous success, it would be that he had magnetism. This applies to almost all the great leaders and Vince certainly was a great leader."

— *Earl (Red) Blaik*

"When he said 'You were chosen to be a Packer,' he made it sound like something unique and wonderful."

— *Willie Davis*

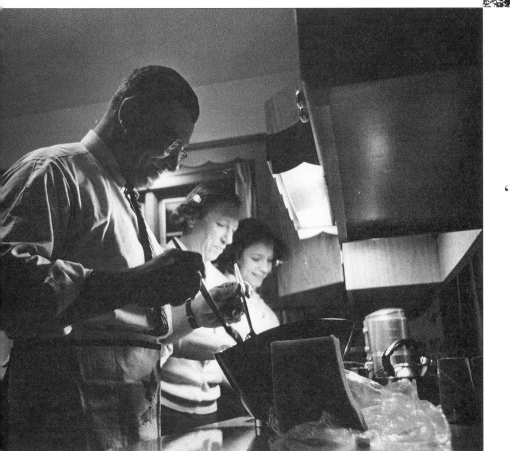

"In great attempts, it is glorious even to fail."

— *Vincent Lombardi*

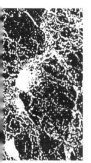

"When all is said and done, a leader must exercise an effective influence and the degree he accomplishes this depends upon the personality of the man. The incandescence of which he is capable; the flame which burns within him; the magnetism which draws the hearts of men toward him."

— *Vincent Lombardi*

"There were times when you'd hear guys say they hated him. But I don't think they really did. They hated the things he made them do. He was making them play better than they were capable of."

— Max McGee

41

INTENSITY

"One day, Marie drove him to practice and a friend went along for the ride. The friend sat in the front seat between Vince and Marie. Vince didn't say a word during the ride, he was so intent, thinking about football. When he reached the stadium, he opened the car door, turned and said, 'Thanks, Honey,' and kissed the guy sitting next to him."

— Bill Austin

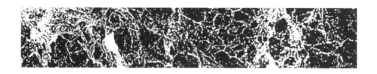

42

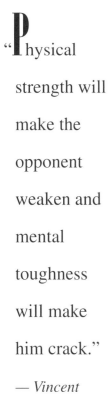

"Physical strength will make the opponent weaken and mental toughness will make him crack."

— *Vincent Lombardi*

43

"**M**ental toughness is essential to success."

— *Vincent Lombardi*

"I know for a fact that there were a few times on the sidelines when he'd get so mad that he'd literally pass out and need oxygen."

— *Vincent Lombardi Jr.*

"His enthusiasm, his spirit, was infectious."

— *Frank Gifford*

45

"You never win a game unless you beat the guy in front of you. The score on the board doesn't mean a thing. That's for the fans. You've got to win the war with the man in front of you. You've got to get your man."

— *Vincent Lombardi*

"It was a helluva performance to listen to when he'd go out there and get his troops around him. He laughed. He cried. He prayed. He motivated. I think he could motivate almost anybody to do almost anything. He communicated with human emotions."

— *Chuck Lane*

"After he would have a horrendous scene with some player in which he would just lace him, he would be emotionally debilitated. He would be exhausted and he'd feel terrible about having done it. He wouldn't have regretted that he'd done it. He would just feel terrible that he had to do it."

— *Edward Bennett Williams*

"No matter how mad he got, he never stopped thinking. That's something. His mind always was going. And it seemed like the more angry he got the harder his mind worked. Maybe anger made his mind better."

— *Mark Duncan*

"The important thought is that the Packers thrived on tough competition. We welcomed it; the team had always welcomed it. The adrenaline flowed a little quicker when we were playing the tougher teams."

— *Vincent Lombardi*

"Those pep talks of his! I was 36 years old and thought I had a little

sophistication, but when I heard those pep talks, I'd cry and go out

49

and try to kill people. Nobody else could do that to me."

— *Emlen Tunnel*

LOVE

"He talked about that word love, but the way he talked about love was a love of peoples' weaknesses. He used to say, 'Everybody can like somebody's strengths and somebody's good looks. But can you like somebody's weaknesses? Can you accept him for his inabilities? That's what we have to do. That's what love is. It is not just the good things.' He used to stress that."

— *Bob Skoronski*

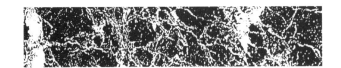

"You can respect a man without personally liking him, but I don't think you can personally like a man without respecting him. Count me among those who personally liked Vince Lombardi."

— *Kyle Rote*

"**H**e had a hard exterior but he also had a big, soft heart."

— *Ray Nitschke*

"**H**eart power is the strength of your company. Heart power is the strength of the Green Bay Packers. Heart power is the strength of America."

— *Vincent Lombardi*

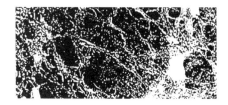

"They may not love you at the time, but they will later."

— *Vincent Lombardi*

"He was very much interested in the total man as far as his players were concerned. I know that he was very interested in the fact that guys be total citizens. In other words, that we not only be good football players and winners, but that we be the type of people, citizens the town would be proud of. He also taught us unselfishness and brotherly love."

— *Carroll Dale*

53

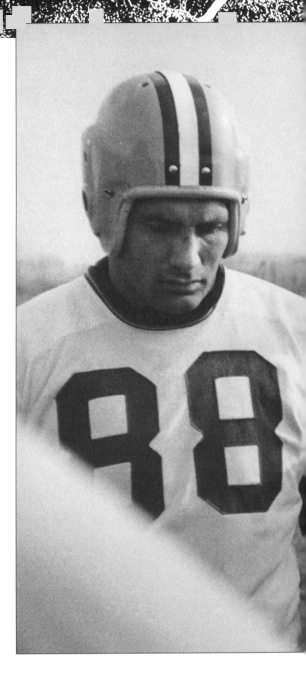

"He was always a
great psychologist,
great at analyzing
individuals,
knowing which
players needed to
be driven and
which ones needed
a friendly pat on
the fanny."

— Frank Gifford

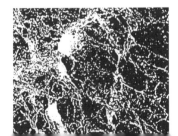

"Only three things should matter to you: your religion, your family and the Green Bay Packers. In that order."

— *Vincent Lombardi*

55

LEADERSHIP

"A leader must be honest with himself and know that as a leader he is just like everybody else. He must identify himself with the group, must back up the group, even at the risk of displeasing superiors. He must believe that the group wants from him a sense of approval. If this feeling prevails, production, discipline, morale will be high, and in return, you can demand the cooperation to promote the goals of the company."

— *Vincent Lombardi*

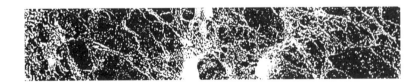

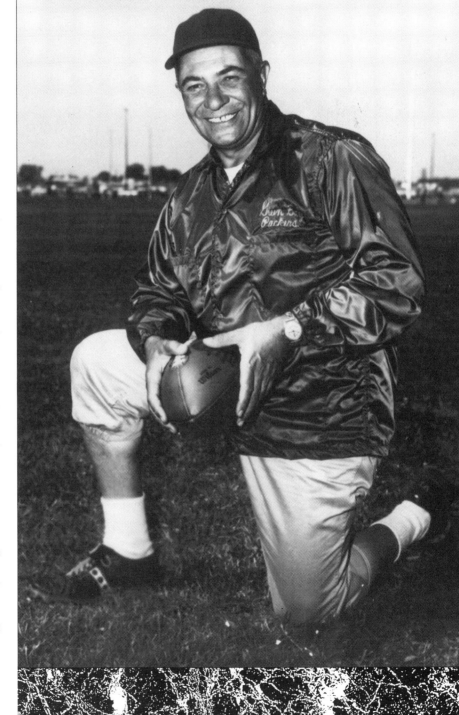

"If Vince Lombardi was a ditch digger, in about two or three weeks, he'd be the foreman, and six weeks later, he'd own the company. He'd be on top. It's the only place he belongs."

— *Bill Austin*

"Leadership rests not only upon ability, not only upon capacity; having the capacity to lead is not enough. The leader must be willing to use it. His leadership is then based on truth and character. There must be truth in the purpose and willpower in the character."

— *Vincent Lombardi*

"He didn't push; he led."
— *Henry Jordan*

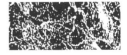

"**H**e was an innovator, willing to experiment to make his team more effective."

— *Merv Hyman*

"**L**eadership is based on a spiritual quality;
the power to inspire, the power to
inspire others to follow."

— *Vincent Lombardi*

59

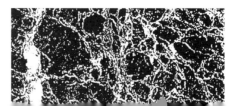

"Some of the things he
had to force himself to do because he
believed they would help us."

— *Hawg Hanner*

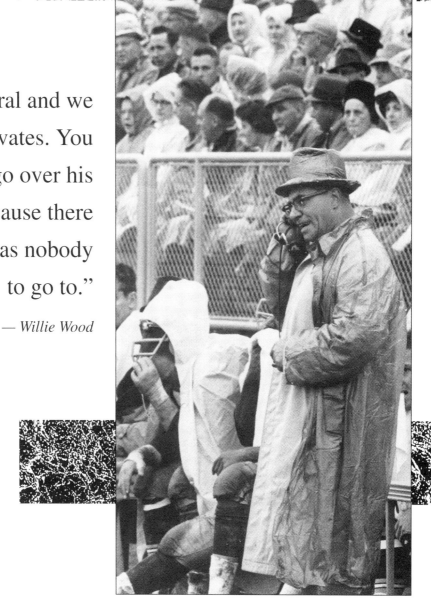

"He was the general and we were the privates. You didn't ever go over his head because there was nobody to go to."

— *Willie Wood*

"He was a commander in the truest sense of the word."

— *Earl Blaik*

61

TEAMWORK

"Teamwork is what the Green Bay Packers were all about. They didn't do it for individual glory. They did it because they loved one another."

— *Vincent Lombardi*

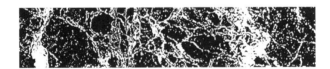

62

"He told us we were going to be a team. We were going to rise and fall on our faces together."

— *Sonny Jurgensen*

"We had as much unity as you could possibly have, which goes along with the love aspect he always talked about."

— *Jim Taylor*

"It was suffering together that made the Packers a great team. And Vince made them suffer."

— *Tom Landry*

"Teams do not go physically flat, they go mentally stale."

— *Vincent Lombardi*

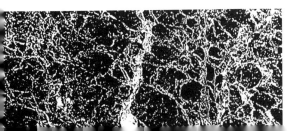

"Individual commitment to a group effort—that is what makes a team, a company work, a society work, a civilization work."

— Vincent Lombardi

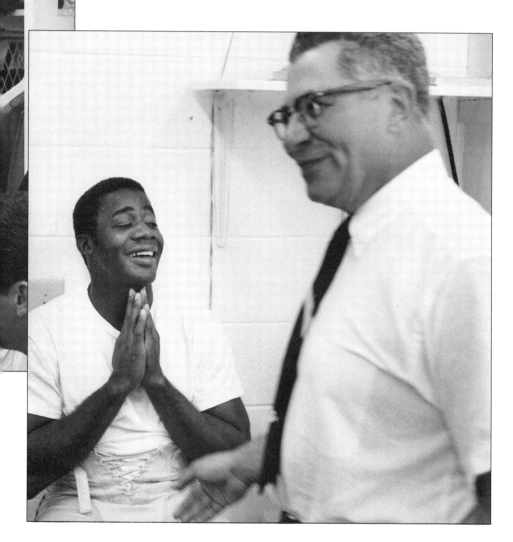

"A leader must believe in teamwork through participation. He can never close the gap between himself and the group. He must walk, as it were, a tightrope between the consent he must win and the control he must exert."

— Vincent Lombardi

SACRIFICE

"To achieve success, whatever the job we have, we must pay a price for success. It's like anything worthwhile. It has a price. You have to pay the price to win and you have to pay the price to get to the point where success is possible. Most important, you must pay the price to stay there."

— *Vincent Lombardi*

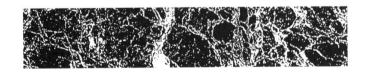

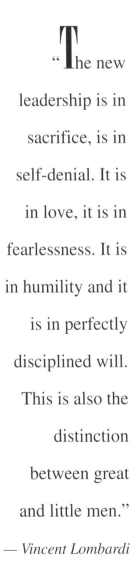

"The new leadership is in sacrifice, is in self-denial. It is in love, it is in fearlessness. It is in humility and it is in perfectly disciplined will. This is also the distinction between great and little men."

— *Vincent Lombardi*

"The team must be molded into a unit, must have a character absolutely of its own, without, in any way, affecting the enormous value of personal aggressiveness or pride."

— *Vincent Lombardi*

"For all who make it, there's got to be a selflessness, a sublimination, automatically, of the individual to the whole."

— *Vincent Lombardi*

"Football is a great deal like life in that it teaches that work, sacrifice, perseverance, competitive drive, selflessness and respect for authority is the price that each and every one of us must pay to achieve any goal that is worthwhile."

— *Vincent Lombardi*

69

INTEGRITY

"Respect wasn't a one way street with him. He demanded it of others but he also gave it."

— *Pete Rozelle*

"What guided him most was fair play. He coached and he did everything with that in mind— recognition of the other man. In other words, you could almost use the word justice."

— *Father David Rondou*

71

"**T**he man who didn't get a fair shake from Vince Lombardi had better look at himself again."

— *Jim Ringo*

"**H**e kind of encouraged his image as a rock— tough and pious."

— *Jimmy Cannon*

"**I**t was religion in the morning and the language of a longshoreman in the afternoon."

— *Jerry Burns*

72

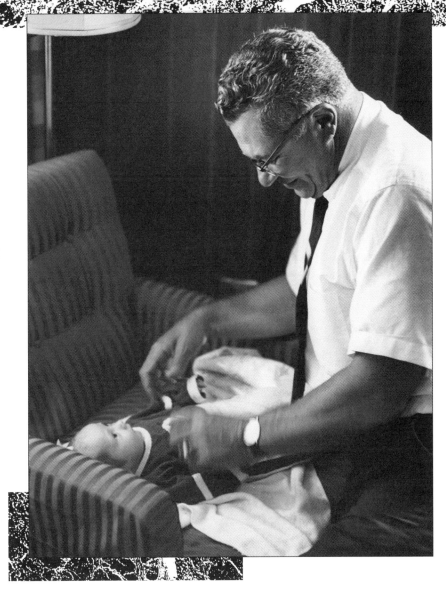

"I loved him because of his total absence of hypocrisy. I loved him because he was the best there ever was at what he did. I loved him because he had the curious capacity for making young men responsive to him without their feeling they had been abused."

— *Howard Cosell*

"When he was trying to convince you he did it with his mind rather than the force of his personality. He had that great logic."

— *Mike Manuche*

73

FEAR

"When Lombardi said 'sit down' we didn't look for a chair."

— *Forrest Gregg*

"He wanted you to stand up to him, to fight back. When he'd get mad at someone, he'd go back in his office and he'd say, 'I wish that son of a bitch would stand up and say what he thinks!' Very few people ever took him up on that offer."

— *Sam Huff*

"He treated us all the same.
Like dogs."

—*Henry Jordan*

"I maintain

that there are

two driving

forces in

football, and

one is anger,

and the other

is fear, and

Lombardi

capitalized on

both of them."

76

—*Willie Davis*

"**I**'ve been written up as a beast, as a lot of things. I don't know what I am."

—*Vincent Lombardi*

"**Y**ou didn't know how the guy was going to react to anything. It kept you off balance. It kept your mind working. Even when you thought he was probably treating you poorly he was probably actually helping you because he kept your mind active. That can't hurt."

— *Lionel Aldridge*

77

"He was tough and abusive and at times he was downright nasty."

— *Bart Starr*

"You knew that if you goofed you were going to catch hell for it."

— *Forrest Gregg*

"Lombardi raises Hell."

— *Paul Hornung*

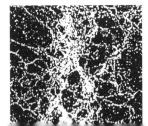

"He would holler at you and harass you so much that you would say to yourself: 'You'd better not blow it or it's all over for you.'"

— *Tom Brown*

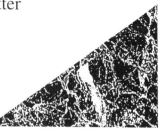

"He made you feel like a million bucks right after you felt like two cents a minute before."

— *Joe Blair*

79

"**O**h, he was tough. Some of the students at St. Cecilia's were a little afraid of him. In fact, sometimes I was a little afraid of him."

— *Father Timothy Moore*

"**I**t was like in the Old Testament, the rule of fear. It was like he was omnipotent and omnipresent. But it was effective."

— *Chuck Lane*

"The fear in my mind was not him but that for some reason I would not be a part of this team and be with this man."

— *Forrest Gregg*

"When I left the Packers, I said that he coached by fear. Later, I thought about it and now I can look back and realize that the reason I resented him was that he was making me grow up when I didn't want to. He was thinking of me."

—*Bill Curry*

81

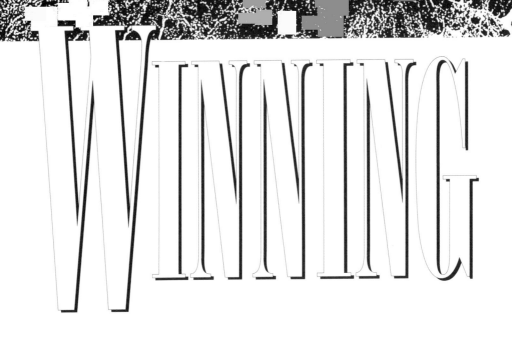

WINNING

"Winning is not a sometime thing; it's an all the time thing. You don't win once in a while; you don't do the right thing once in awhile; you do them right all the time. Winning is a habit. Unfortunately, so is losing."

— *Vincent Lombardi*

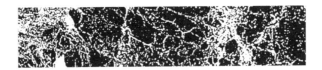

"Winning the first time is a lot easier than repeating as champions. To succeed again requires dedication, perseverance and, above all, discipline and mental toughness."

— *Vincent Lombardi*

"**Y**ou never lose.
But sometimes the clock
runs out on you."

— *Vincent Lombardi*

"**S**ome of us
will do our jobs
well and some
will not, but
we will all be
judged by only
one thing—
the result."

— *Vincent Lombardi*

"Success is a habit. Winning is a habit. Unfortunately, so is losing."

— *Vincent Lombardi*

"People are always asking me what made Vince Lombardi different from other coaches, and I've got one answer: He could get that extra 10 percent out of an individual. Multiply ten percent times forty men on a team times fourteen games a season and you're going to win."

— *Frank Gifford*

85

"He could have made a success out of the Edsel."

— *Sonny Jurgensen*

"I firmly believe that any man's finest hour—his greatest fulfillment to all he holds dear—is that moment when he has worked his heart out in a good cause and lies exhausted on the field of battle—victorious."

— *Vincent Lombardi*

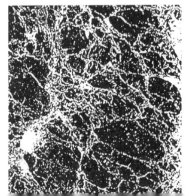

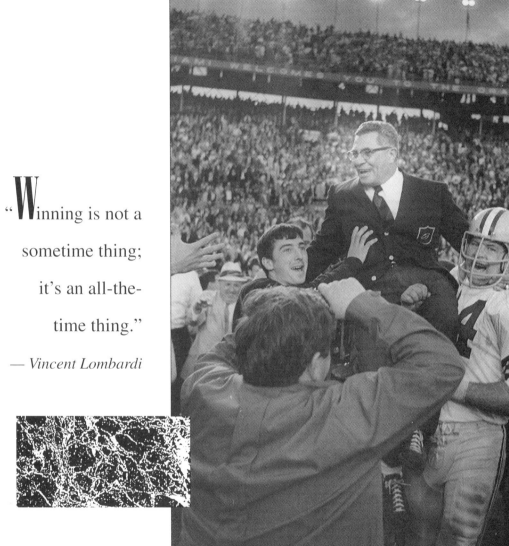

"Winning is not a
sometime thing;
it's an all-the-
time thing."

— *Vincent Lombardi*

"If you can accept losing, you can't win."

— *Vincent Lombardi*

"Winning is not everything— but making the effort to win is."

— *Vincent Lombardi*

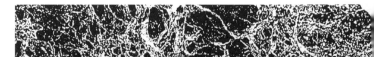

Other Books From Celebrating Excellence

Commitment to Excellence

Management Magic

Business Quotes

Motivational Quotes

Customer Care

Opportunity Selling

The Best of Success

Great Quotes from Great Leaders

Great Quotes from Great Women

Commitment to Quality

Zig Ziglar's Favorite Quotations

Winning With Teamwork

The Power of Goals

Your Attitude Determines Your Altitude

Never, Never Quit

CELEBRATING EXCELLENCE PUBLISHING